P 10

TRISTAN AND ISOLDE

TRISTAN AND ISOLDE

from a manuscript of
"The Romance of Tristan"
(15 th century)

Introduction by
Dagmar Thoss

Text by
Gabriel Bise

Liber

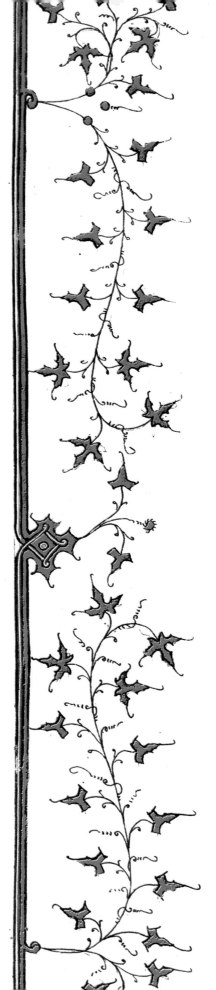

This book is illustrated with miniatures taken from the Roman de Tristan, a French manuscript of the early 15th century, one of the numerous treasures of the National Library of Austria. They describe the episodes of the story of Tristan and Isolde—whence the title of the book.

Vienna, Austrian National Library, Ms. 2537.
Photos: Austrian National Library.

The publishers are sincerely grateful to Pr.-Dr. Otto Mazal, Keeper of the Department of Manuscripts at the National Library of Austria, and to his assistant, Dr. Eva Irblich, for their kind and valuable cooperation.

A MANUSCRIPT OF THE PROSE VERSION OF "TRISTAN" SUMPTUOUSLY ILLUSTRATED BY THE MASTER OF BEDFORD, FROM THE LIBRARY OF THE DUC DE BERRY.

The illuminated Codex and Jean, duc de Berry.

The Vienna Manuscript Codex 2537, which contains a greatly amplified version of the Tristan legend, enriched by a wealth of additional episodes and narratives—known for short as the "Prose Tristan"—is, in purely quantitative terms, a prodigious work. The book is 19 inches long, 14 inches wide and 492 parchment pages thick. But what is special about it is its rich artistry, above all the 144 miniatures, some of which are of outstanding quality.

A luxurious codex such as this raises questions as to the precise historical conditions under which it was created, and especially who might have commissioned such a spendidly illustrated manuscript. Normally such a manuscript gives indications as to the identity of its original owner, whether by means of coats of arms or family mottos, which are often a part of the presentation and appear in margins or miniatures, or an owner's mark at the beginning or end of the codex. In many cases entries in account books survive by chance to indicate who commissioned the work and often even who the artists were; valuable clues are also sometimes provided by inventories. This particular illuminated manuscript seemed at first to offer no basis for the identification of the original owner, and thus the time and place of its creation could be ascertained only in very general terms. Indeed, it was done mainly on the basis of the history of art: the decoration and pictorial elements could be located as Parisian on the grounds of general stylistic developments (of which more will be said later) and dated in the early fifteenth century, about 1410. In the case of this type of de luxe secular manuscript one could assume that the patron was a member of the higher nobility.

A recently discovered signature has finally made it possible to identify the original owner: none other than Jean, duc de Berry, one of the greatest bibliophiles of his time. His handwriting was discovered at the end of the book on folio 492^r, underneath the last line of text *(le romant de tristan et de yseult)*. In this place the blank parchment was slightly thinner and somewhat roughened, as is the case when erasing has been done with a scraping knife to remove the top layer of parchment. Under ultra-violet light, which picked up particles of ink which had penetrated more deeply into the parchment, fragments of writing appeared (fig. p. 11) which can faintly but decipherably be recognized as *Ce livre est au duc de Berry*, that is an owner's mark, and *JEhanB*, the signature of the duc de Berry. As the Vienna signature is difficult to reproduce, for the sake of clarity it can be compared with that in a codex in Paris (Ms. fr. 5707, folio 367ʳ)[fig. p. 11]: the letters *JEhanB* which are clearly legible there are almost completely extant in the Vienna codex, for example, the tiny wavy lines and somewhat higher initial stroke of the *J*, the upper limit of the *h*; the final *B*, terminating in its characteristic long rising half-circle, can be recognized clearly, as can other features. In the Paris manuscript the owner's manuscript mark which follows it on the left, *Ceste bible est au duc de Berry...* corresponds closely to the mark in the Vienna codex—a point which can be seen clearly in detail; in the latter it crowns the signature in a gently curving arch.

Thus the Vienna manuscript came from one of the richest and most precious libraries of all time, that of Jean de France, duc de Berry (1340-1416), the son, brother and uncle respectively of the French kings Jean II the Good (reigning 1350-1364), Charles V the Wise (1364-1380) and Charles VI (1380-1422). He was, moreover, brother to Louis I, duc d'Anjou, to Philip the Bold, duc de Bourgogne, and to Isabelle of France, who married Gian B. Galeazzo Visconti, duke of Milan. They were without exception great bibliophiles. Jean de Berry's mother, Bonne of Luxembourg, commissioned works by Jean Pucelle, the greatest miniaturist of the first half of the 14th century; his father, Jean the Good, even purchased books while a prisoner of war in England during the Hundred Years' War. His brother, King Charles V, had a thousand books (in those days a huge library) extending over every field of knowledge. To house it he arranged his own permanent library in the Louvre, and thus provided the nucleus of the Royal Library, which later became the Bibliothèque Nationale. This collection was only slightly superior to that of the duke's sister, Isabella, and of his brother-in-law, Gian Galleazzo Visconti. Similarly, his other two brothers, the dukes of Anjou and Bourgogne, owned many manuscripts with or without illuminations.

But the library of Jean de Berry surpassed all the others, not in quantity (at the time of the second inventory, in 1413-16, there were close on 300 books) but in richness and splendor of artistry. Almost half of them were manuscripts with miniatures executed by the best artists of the age or of the period before it. Jean de Berry was tireless in his efforts to engage the exclusive services of outstanding artists at his court or to give them individual commissions. The former was the case with the Limbourg brothers, who worked almost exclusively for the duc de Berry and in their depictions of landscapes and châteaux showed a previously unknown level of realism. Their treatment of scenes, too, developed a new power of dramatic narration. Individual commissions were given to artists from the Bedford-Boucicaut studio, leading painters of their age. The Boucicaut Master was, moreover, a pioneer in the organization of pictorial space. Jean de Berry not only commissioned new manuscripts, he was constantly searching for extant codices with rich illustrations. A number of dealers worked to find them under his orders. At the death of the bibliophiles Charles V and Louis d'Orléans, the duke himself attended to the matter in person. He was also very adept at contriving to be presented with books, or he would borrow several and keep them for such a length of time that they were only returned after his death. (Sumptuously illustrated books were quite often given as presents, especially at New Year. Thus Berry and Bourgogne, closely related, would regularly send each other rich gifts, especially valuable books, despite their violent political conflicts).

That the aesthetic element played a major if not a decisive role in the duc de Berry's collecting mania can be judged for instance from the titles of some of his many devotional works; their titles are *Belles* Heures, *Très Belles* Heures, *Très Belles* Heures de Notre-Dame, *Très Riches* Heures, *Grandes* Heures — their nomenclature is according to the level of artistic excellence. The "Grande Heures" have a format (16 × 12 inches) totally unsuitable for a layman's prayer book; the religious text was merely the occasion for a kind of small picture gallery in the form of whole-page miniatures.

Inventories made during the duke's lifetime (1401-03 and 1413-16) and thereafter (1416) give us an extremely accurate idea of the treasures he possessed. On this basis it has been possible to ascertain that about a third of all his books have survived. Here one must bear in mind that manuscripts are known which, though they bear his signature, do not appear in the inventories (a fact explained by the already mentioned custom of giving presents and by the frequent borrowing of books, both factors which must have caused considerable

laisse le conte a pler et retourne a tristan et a gouuernal qui sont ou royaume de loenois en la compaigne de la royne qui estoit maraistre de tristan.

R dit le conte que apres la mort du roy meliadus demoura tristan en loenois vne espace de téps auecques la royne sa maraistre et gouuernal aussi qui moult diligément et auieusement nourrissoit et gardoit son nourrisson tristan. Si se apperceut gouuernal asse[z] briefment que la royne pourchacoit de tout son pouoir la mort de tristan. Et pour certain si trauoit elle de tout son pouoir ne nattendoit fors heure et temps quelle le veust faire si le

fluctuations in the contents of individual libraries). Nor is the Vienna Tristan manuscript to be found in any of the inventories. As it was only recently recognized as having belonged to Jean de Berry, it increases the contents of the original library and of its surviving elements by one magnificent manuscript. For the Vienna Tristan manuscript itself there is now a *terminus ante quem* of 1413 for its leaving the Berry library and consequently for its creation, as it does not appear in the inventory kept regularly from 1413 onwards. The manuscript, which on stylistic grounds cannot have been created much before 1410, must therefore have left the library soon after its completion and painting. A later owner then erased the signature and mark of the duc de Berry. (As so often happens, we are largely in the dark as to how this manuscript came into the hands of its present owner. At the beginning of the 18th century it appeared in the library of Eugene Prince of Savoy, where it received the Baroque binding which it has to this day—fine red kid with the gold leaf armorial bearings and monogram of its owner. After the death of Eugene of Savoy, the Emperor, Karl VI of Austria, acquired his entire rich library, which is today one of the most important manuscript components of the Austrian National Library.)

Jean de Berry's inventories also make it possible to assess more closely the importance of his bibliophilia and thus of the individual richly illustrated codices within the range of his considerably broader collecting habits. Thus we note his constant search for precious stones—rubies, sapphires, emeralds and diamonds, of which several were already famous because of their extraordinary size and which in magnificent settings of gold and pearls served as personal jewellery, adorned costly bindings or were incorporated in secular and religious works of art. His collection of cut stones, gems and cameos dating from antiquity or in the form of medieval copies was widely known. He also owned antique coins and medallions which, though contemporary, were worked in the ancient styles. To the objects of antiquity and pseudo-antiquity can be added Byzantine works of art. Nor did he lack relics; but here too, as has already been noted in the case of his Books of Hours, the religious and devotional aspect must not be over-estimated, as reliquaries served rather as an opportunity for artistic creation and the magnificent use of rich materials. The secular element of the reliquary, the

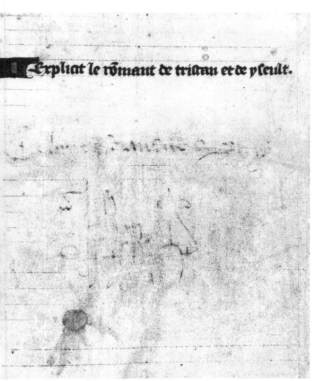
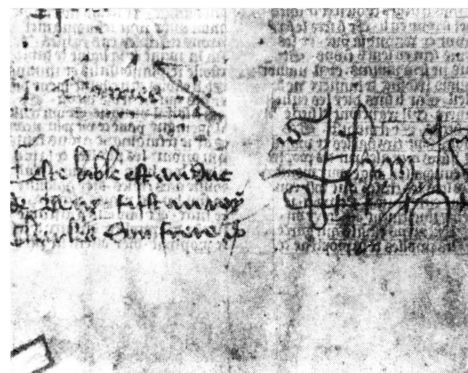

Signatures of the Duke de Berry
(Left, Ms. of Vienna; right, Ms. of Paris).

objet d'art for its own sake, was the main thing.

However, the collecting activities of Jean de Berry took on even greater, almost absurd dimensions: over seventeen châteaux, palaces and fine country houses in Berry, Poitou, the Auvergne and in and around Paris were continually being built, altered or extended: they were architectural jewels. To mention only one example, the château of Mehun-sur-Yèvre, near Bourges, was famous far and wide. Philip the Bold, the mighty duke of Burgundy, sent his artists to see its splendors. In the "Très Riches Heures" of the Limburg brothers, which surpasses all other Books of Hours, the château of Mehun-sur-Yèvre is shown, in the scene of Christ's temptation by the Devil, as the embodiment of all earthly treasures. The duke progressed luxuriously from one residence to another, always accompanied by a large retinue and with an extravagant train, of which, for example, even bears (one of the duke's emblems) formed a part. Entire interior décors accompanied him on his travels, spendidly woven and embroidered tapestries, ceiling-cloths and leather hangings, equally precious tableware and cutlery. Secular and religious festivals and ceremonies were celebrated with much pomp and expense.

It is difficult to find a common denominator for the duke's art-related activities and the artistic patronage connected with it, unless it be that its extraordinary variety (always in extremely costly settings and in a selection which aimed at the highest quality and extended to all aspects of life), in unison with the highest forms of magnificence, became a way of life.

Of course, all this had to be financed. Very early on, Jean, a king's son, received Poitou from the hands of his father, Jean the Good, as a fief. When he lost this to England in the Hundred Years' War he received in its place Auvergne and Berry. Later Poitou was returned to him after it was won back from the English by skilful negotiations. Thus Jean was Duke of Berry, of the Auvergne, Count of Poitou and Etampes, and, moreover, Governor of Languedoc. Consequently a large part of what is today central and southern France paid taxes to the duke, a fact which he richly exploited. Rebellions caused by oppressive taxation were no rarity: their suppression was immediately followed by further, and this time punitive taxes. Such happenings were not confined to the territories actually administered by the duc de Berry.

— Isolde

At the time when he conducted affairs of state jointly with the duc de Bourgogne during the minority of Charles VI, the rebellion of the Maillotins was put down by both dukes and punished by enormous fines. Violent protests made Charles VI, after he had begun his reign, relieve the duc de Berry, his uncle, of financial responsibility for Languedoc.

Of all this breathtaking splendor little now remains. Even during the lifetime of the duc de Berry part of his treasures were lost to him. His political unskillfulness, particularly in the conflicts which arose out of the political aspirations of the dukes of Burgundy, led to the plundering of his Paris residence, the Hôtel de Nesle, and the burning of his château de Bicêtre, south of Paris, in the course of which incalculable riches were lost. When in consequence of these clashes the duc de Bourgogne and Charles VI besieged their uncle, Jean de Berry, in Bourges, the latter was forced to melt down the *objets d'art* formerly bequeathed to the Sainte Chapelle there, including retables of solid gold, jewel-studded crosses, richly ornamented reliquaries, etc., in order to find gold with which to pay his troops. Payment of reparations to England further decreased the duc de Berry's stock of precious and artistically wrought jewels. After the death of the duc de Berry the majority of his moveable chattels were dispersed to the four winds. Creditors claimed their share, as Jean de Berry, in his insatiable desire for precious things, had run deep into debt, despite his enormous income. Of his many châteaux only a few sad remnants survive. And even those parts that withstood the depredations of war, of weather, and of demolition for use as building materials—such as the Sainte Chapelle in Bourges—fell victim to the French Revolution.

Today hardly anything survives of all that incredible luxury and immense splendor. The only things to have come to us, at least in part, are the precious, richly ornamented and illustrated manuscripts. In the protective isolation of libraries they were less exposed to the ravages of time. Not being made of bullion or precious stones they could not be re-used for another purpose. They were equally insignificant from a political point of view, as they (unlike the châteaux) were not symbols of power visible from afar. One of these remaining testimonies to departed glories is the Vienna Prose Tristan.

— *Tristan*

The artistry of the codex and its miniaturists.

Miniatures are often viewed disparagingly as a minor art form. This attitude is generally incorrect, and, as regards the period around 1400—the object of our special interest here—is totally mistaken. Especially in the Gothic period in France, as in Europe north of the Alps generally, painting was almost synonymous with glass and miniature painting. Glass used in windows and parchment used in codices were the most important materials for pictorial art. There were not yet as many panel paintings as in later periods, whilst fresco painting had declined in comparison with the Romanesque period, as Gothic cathedrals had no walls suitable for this form of art.

So in the period about 1400, when in court circles, for example in Paris and the residences of the duc de Berry, the exquisite, tiny but spendidly and sumptuously executed works of art were seen as aesthetically desirable, miniatures and book paintings were the most congenial form of artistic expression. Jean de Berry even had miniatures executed by a sculptor (Beauneveu). In those days the highest achievements of painting were seen in miniatures; the greatest and most influential painters of the age were illustrators (the Limbourg brothers, Masters of Boucicaut, etc.). The miniature was a high art form.

Jean de Berry's wide collecting interests and the variety and heterogeneity of the *objets d'art* available to him can also be seen in his choice of artists. For the adornment of his books he employed all and sundry without regard to their stylistic tendencies, subject to one condition only, that their artistic quality matched his high standards. Thus it was that the best and most eminent illustrators of his age worked for him. He succeeded in attaching some to his court, as in the case of the Limbourg brothers who originally worked for the Burgundian Philip the Bold, but then devoted themselves exclusively to the service of their new patron. Others worked in their own private studios in Paris, as did the Master of the Duke of Bedford and that of the Marshal of Boucicaut. Their miniatures thus appear in the manuscripts of a variety of patrons, including those of the duc de Berry, as the Vienna Tristan Codex shows.

The artistic atmosphere at the court of the king of France

and those of the various dukes was decidedly cosmopolitan. In the course of the 14th century an uninterrupted exchange of artistic ideas took place all over Europe. Among the areas taking part were Italian cities, Avignon, residence of the pope, Prague, the residence of the German emperor, and the French courts, primarily the king's court at Paris and that of the duc de Bourgogne at Dijon. Moreover France attracted artists from the Netherlands and the Rhineland (the principal master of the Vienna Tristan Codex was in all probability of Netherlandish origin). About 1400 there was a general unification of artistic forms of expression, so that the origin of a master and the place where a work of art was executed were no longer of much significance and indeed were sometimes hard to discern. Thus, too, we see the emergence at this time of a universal style, which transcended local and national demarcation lines, and is known as the "International Style", or the "Courtly Style circa 1400".

This style is the prerequisite for the miniature art of the Tristan Codex. It shows itself in the curving lines of the composition, a feature which extends to most of the figures or groups of figures which have a characteristic inclination of the head and a gentle downwards flowing line of draperies extending to the ground (for example, folio 56^r, cf. fig. p. 36), or in the lengthened proportions and stylized attitudes of certain of the figures (for example the one on the far left of the same miniature). But the figures of the principal master do not show the elongation and mannered curve of the body so absolutely, in part his figures are firmer, more compact and more natural in their movements. Colors are no longer purely decorative in character, but are more somber, and the jewel-like brilliance characteristic of the "International Style" is subdued. Thus the miniatures of the principal master of the Vienna Tristan Codex show features of style which diverge slightly from the "International Style", inasmuch as it contains elements which only became pronounced during the following period. The miniaturist with whom we are concerned here executed the most important works in the Codex, the four-part miniature at the beginning (folio 4^r; cf. fig. p. 17) and the three-part one at the end (folio 474v; cf. fig. p. 120/ 122) as well as a number of other pictures, especially in the first part of the book. The correspondences of style between these miniatures and those of the Master of the Duke of Bedford—seen best in the habits of composition, types of face and figure, facial expressions, characteristic attitudes, peculiarities of modelling, treatment of landscape elements, etc.—

makes it possible to discern the hand of this miniaturist in them also. The actual name of this artist is not known; he is named after his patron, John, Duke of Bedford, for whom he executed two of his most important and extensive works, a Book of Hours in the British Library (British Museum, Add. MS 18550) and a breviary in the Bibliothèque Nationale, Paris (Ms. lat. 17924). The Duke of Bedford, brother of King Henry V of England, was the English commander during the siege of Paris and was a great patron of the arts there for many years.

As with most works ascribed to this artist, both the codices mentioned above were created later than our Tristan manuscript: the Book of Hours dates from the first half of the fourteen-twenties, and the breviary was not yet completed in 1435, on the death of the Duke of Bedford. On the basis of other Books of Hours (Vienna, Austrian National Library, Codex 1855; Lisbon, Gulbenkian Collection; Fort Worth, Arthur Haddaway Collection; Yale University, Beinecke Library, MS 400) this style can be traced to the second decade of the fifteenth century, which approximates more closely to the date of the Tristan codex. In attempting to date this miniaturist around the beginning of the 15th century on formal grounds, one is confronted by a problem, common in the history of art, namely the identification of the early work of an artist whose maturer period is completely known. As a connecting link between the well known Bedford style, which remained homogeneous over a relatively long period, and the new elements of an emerging personal artistic style, the miniatures of the Tristan manuscript are of an importance which must not be under-estimated. It contains a sizeable cycle of pictures which, on the one hand, can definitely be ascribed to the Master of Bedford, but at the same time because of their absolutely certain dating before 1413, belong to a little known period of this artist, who was so eminent among the Paris illustrators of the early 15th century. Few other codices, or individual miniatures contained in them, can claim such a position of importance: the framework of the title picture of the "Térence des ducs" (1405-10, Paris, Bibliothèque de l'Arsenal, MS 664), a few miniatures in the roughly contemporary "Livre de chasse" by Gaston Phoebus (Paris, Bibliothèque Nationale, ms. fr. 616) and a miniature in the "Grandes Heures du duc de Berry" (Paris, Bibliothèque Nationale Ms. lat. 919).

It has already been pointed out that not all the miniatures in the Vienna Codex are by the same artist: apart from the

Cy comencent li ... de relpien et
wohlir. Tranflatees de latin en francois par
vn noble cheualier dengletie appelle luces li
gneur du chaftel du graut pres de falebie

Pres ce que iay leu et releu
et pourueu par maintefois.
le graut liure de latin celui
meifmes qui deuife appert
ment lyftoire du fait graal
auoult me merueille que
aucun pudome ne bient
auaut qui empreigne a
tranflater le de latin en
francois Car ce feroit vne chofe qui woulent
onuient poures et riches pourquoy ilz euffent
woulente defcouter et deutendre belles auctuues
et pleifans qui amidient en la graut bretain
gue au temps le roy artus et deuant tout auli
comme lyftoire vraye du faint graal qui bien
fait a oute le nous tefmoigne mais quant ie

woy que nuls ne fole empreudre ponire que trop
feroit greueuse chofe ace que trop y auoit afane
rar trop eft graude et merueilleufe lyftoire. Je
luces cheualier et feigneur du chaftel du graut
wifing prochain de falebieres Comme cheualier
amourtreur et enuoilies empriang a tranflater
te latin en francois vne ptie de celle hyftoire non
nue ponire que ie fache graut trauet francois ains
appartient plus ma langue et ma parleure a la
manere dangleterre que a celle de frauce comme
cellui qui fu nez en angleterre mais telle est ma
woulente et mon propofement q ie en langue fran
roife le tranflateray au mieulx que ie pourray
a mon pouoir fans y mettre menfonge mais
la verite toute apperte de monftreray et feray
affanoir ce que ie latin deuife de lyftoire de trif
tan qui fu le plus fouuerain cheualier qui onc
ques fouft ou ropaume de la graut bretaigne
au temps du roy artus ne deuant ne aps fors
feulement galaad le trefbon chlr et lancelot

— *King Mark*

Master of Bedford other miniaturists had a hand in them. The Vienna Tristan is thus an excellent example of a commonly used system for sharing out the work of a long series of illustrations: individual quires or groups of quires (units of a codex consisting of several, usually four, sheets stitched together) were allocated to various artists, so that several miniaturists could work simultaneously on the same manuscript. In this particular cycle of miniatures three stylistic groups can be distinguished, which alternate nine times in all. In each case the stylistic change coincides with the beginning of a new quire. A slight irregularity occurs: in two places, a single miniature in the style of the principal master has been inserted in quires executed by one of his collaborators.

The artists other than the Master of Bedford can also be identified stylistically. One of these can be shown to be a pupil of the principal artist (see folio 259^r and others, cf. fig. p. 82). Overall the miniatures in the Bedford style run from the beginning to folio 19, from folio 28 to 83, 143-190, 354-302 471-474 and additionally 219^r and 239v. The principal collaborators, judged on numerical grounds (in folios 20-

27, 119-142, 191-253 and 303-470) show the influence of the Master of the Berry Apocalypse (MS 133 Pierpont Morgan Library, New York), in whose studio they were evidently trained. This group of miniatures is remarkable for its bright, gay colors, especially in its architecture. The figures have little that is corporeal, their flatly extended robes often spreading down in an outward curve, so that one has the impression that they are suspended in the air rather than standing on the ground (examples of this style can be seen on folios 26v, 233^r, 408v and others; cf. fig. p. 22,77,115). Another artist whose work con be seen in the quires from folio 84 to 118 is of the school of the Master of Luçon (a miniaturist named after a pontifical made for Etienne Loypeau, bishop of Luçon, ms. fr. 8886 in the Bibliothèque Nationale, Paris). These miniatures form the oldest stylistic level in the Vienna Tristan Codex and thus in their facial types, physical attitudes and above all their totally non-spatial setting (compare for example the female figure on folios 103^r and 118^r; cf. figs. p. 47 and p. 49) clearly refer back to the 14th century.

In the field of book illustration, there is another form of

— *Merlin*

work-sharing which became established very early: illustrators commissioned to paint pictures to illustrate narratives— they were known as "historieurs"— were not usually responsible for the decorative elements, initial letters, frameworks, borders and ends of lines. The artists who carried out this type of work were called "enlumineurs". Outstanding examples of their work are to be found in the sumptuous framework of the first four miniatures (folio 4^r; cf. fig. p. 17): a magnificent framework figured in gold and color and a rich border of spiky ivy scrolls surround the miniatures and the text. The large, prominent initial, whose body is formed from different patterns and whose square background is also filled with ivy scrolls, is tied into the framework. In a simplified form this kind of decor is to be found throughout the whole codex, generally being used to emphasize the beginning of a new chapter.

History of the Tristan legend.

The Tristan theme has its origin in the literature of the Celts, that race which before its conquest by the Romans and the Germanic tribes was settled throughout Western Europe. The Celtic race and its language was assimilated or driven out in the course of several centuries and survived only in the border areas of Europe, in Ireland, Wales, Cornwall and Brittany. It was from these regions that numerous Celtic myths, sagas and tales entered French literature in the twelfth century. This came about in two ways. Firstly, by means of oral tradition: from the end of the eleventh century onwards Celtic bards came to the English and French courts and told their stories and *lais*, so that from 1120 the Celtic themes may be assumed to have been generally known. A second important source, especially for the Arthurian legend, was the *History of the Kings of England* ("Historia Regum Britanniae") written in 1135 in Latin by Geoffroy of Monmouth, in which the author expands Breton chronicles into a kind of heroic epic whose main characters are King Arthur and his knights. For French authors of this period the Celtic material represented an inexhaustible reservoir of legends, themes, symbols, mysterious or fantastic things and events which could be freely used and combined. Soon after the middle of the twelfth century the three main themes of

IEAN DE FRANCE DVC DE BERRY.
mort en 1416.

French writing in this field were complete: the story of Tristan and Isolde, the legend of Arthur and that of the Holy Grail. Thanks to the extraordinarily wide cultural influence of France in this period they soon became known and loved throughout Europe.

Of the story of Tristan and Isolde in French literature two versions dating from the second half of the twelfth century have come down to us, both of them incomplete. Although they were written at about the same time, that of Béroul, with its lapidary narrative technique and simpler literary form, approaches closer to the genre of the heroic epic, whilst that of Thomas bears the imprint of purely courtly ideas.

The tendency in French literature of the thirteenth century to adapt subjects already used in verse narratives to the form of prose romances affected large areas of Celtic themes. Here a second factor appears, one of decisive importance for the history of literature, inasmuch as tales which had originally been treated in separate, individual works were now put together in long cycles and harmonized with one another—a process which naturally brought about considerable changes in content and adjustments on all sides. The narrative framework of this gradually developing new "Celtic" cycle is formed by two of the above-mentioned main themes, the Arthurian legend and that of the Holy Grail. The quest for the mysterious Grail provides the main thread of the plot and makes it possible to interweave extremely diverse, parallel and often highly complicated narratives. Time and time again peerless and proven knights set out to find the Grail. In between their long, eventful and adventurous quests they return to the court of King Arthur who, with his knights of the Round Table is the center and at the same time the point of departure of everything that takes place in the story. The Tristan legend, originally unconnected with either King Arthur or with the quest for the Grail, was especially affected by this transformation of the Breton themes by the power of the Arthurian and Grail legends combined in this manner. Though the prose Tristan of circa 1230 was not directly incorporated into the developing cycle, the author took over parts of it and took great care to treat the story of the Arthurian knight who appeared in his work in such a way as to avoid contradictions in the latter's role, position and character in the "cycle". Most importantly, the figure of Tristan is completely absorbed by the new principal themes of the cycle: he becomes one of the knights of the Round Table, spends most of his time as a knight-errant and even takes part in the quest for the Grail. The actual Tristan legend, the story of the fatal love between Tristan and Isolde, plays only a subordinate part in the prose version. The prose Tristan has become mainly an adventurous romance (in the original sense of "roman"). The names of the authors given in the prologue and epilogue—Luce del Gast and Helie de Boron—are not considered historically authentic.

The fact that the early verse versions of the Tristan theme, which were a faithful reflection of the original legend, have been totally lost or survive only in the form of a few fragments without illustrations, whilst we have almost eighty manuscripts, many of them richly illustrated, and eight printed editions of the prose version, can be ascribed to several factors which produced a combined effect in the early decades of the thirteenth century. Up to the end of the 12th century not only epic but even courtly poetry was intended to be listened to rather than read: courtly patrons had stories told to them in preference to reading them in books. Thus an essential motive for the creation of illustrated texts was absent. Moreover, up to the end of the twelfth century, it was the monasteries which were the centers of manuscript production; it was not until the thirteenth century that this role was take over by professional lay studios. This then provided the basis for the great expansion of non-religious art. But at this time, when conditions for the continuance of secular literature, especially in the form of illustrated manuscripts, were so favorable, the older Tristan works had become old-fashioned and were thus no longer copied, as all interest now centered on the new prose romance.

The surviving manuscripts of the prose Tristan are fairly evenly divided between the 13th, 14th and 15th centuries, the period 1400, from which our copy dates, being the zenith of the text's popularity and of its dissemination through the medium of richly illustrated manuscript books.

D.T.

Select bibliography

The historical background: Lehoux, F., *Jean de France, duc de Berri, sa vie, son action politique.* 4 vols., Paris, 1966-68. Meiss, M., *French painting in the time of Jean de Berry; the late fourteenth century and the patronage of the Duke.* London/New York, 1967. The Master of the Duke of Bedford and miniaturists of the period in general: Porcher, J., *L'enluminure française.* Paris, 1959. Spencer, E., *The Master of the Duke of Bedford: The Bedford Hours,* in Burlington Magazine 107 (1965), pp. 495-502. Meiss, M., *French painting in the time of Jean de Berry, the late fourteenth century and the patronage of the Duke.* London/New York, 1967. Meiss, M., *The Boucicaut Master,* London/New York, 1968. Meiss, M., *The Limbourgs and their contemporaries.* London/New York, 1974. Meiss, M., *The de Lévis Hours and the Bedford Workshop,* New Haven, 1972. See also the review by J.J.G. Alexander, *Masters and their methods,* in Times Literary Supplement, 24.9.76. The Tristan theme: Loseth, E., *Le Roman en prose de Tristan, le Roman de Palamedes et la compilation de Rusticien de Pise.* Paris, 1891. Loomis, R.S., *Arthurian Legends in medieval art.* London, 1938. Curtis, R.L., *Le Roman de Tristan en prose,* vol. I Munich, 1963. The Vienna manuscript: Hermann, H.J., *Französische und iberische Handschriften der ersten Hälfte des 15. Jahrhunderts* (Beschreibendes Verzeichnis der illuminierten Handschriften in Osterreich, N.F., Band VII/3). Leipzig, 1938, pp. 44-64. Thoss, D., *Ein Prosa Tristan aus dem Beistz des Duc de Berry in der Österreichischen Nationalbibliothek* (Cod. 2537), in Codices Manuscripti 3 (1977), pp. 66-72. *Französische Gotik und Renaissance in Meisterwerken der Buchmalerei,* Catalogue of the Exhibition of Collections of Manuscripts and Incunabilia of the Austrian National Library, Vienna, 1978, 103-105.

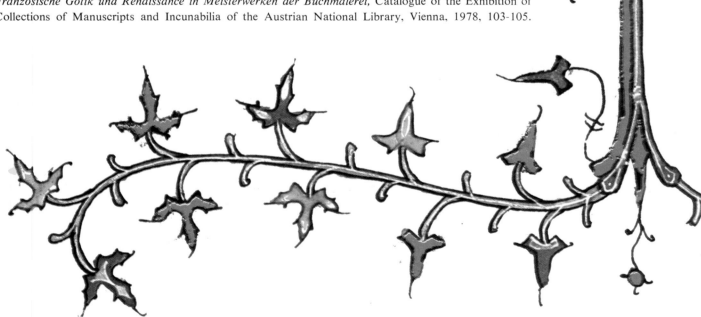

Abandoned and grief-stricken in the depths of the forest, Elizabeth, Queen of Lyoness, died while giving birth to her child Tristan; his very name suggests the sadness of the circumstances surrounding his birth. The baby was found by his father, King Meladius, brother-in-law of King Mark of Cornwall, and taken back to the court, where he spent his childhood, an orphan showered with every conceivable attention by all those around him. However, he was a prince of the royal blood, and accordingly had to undergo the training which would make of him a valiant knight. The king consulted his soothsayer, the magician Merlin, the omniscient prophet who had emerged from the depths of the forests of Brittany, and whose magic powers enabled him to appear simultaneously in the most unlikely places. In this way it was decided that the man to teach the prince the martial arts and act as his tutor was Curvenal, one of the wisest and most loyal of the royal squires. Then, amongst the flower-beds of the park next to the royal castle, under the indulgent gaze of Merlin, Curvenal, wearing his magnificent ceremonial cloak, kneeled before the king and received from him the child who, under his tutelage, was to become the valiant and loyal Tristan, hero of countless feats of arms.

When he was not away at the wars with his men, or competing at tournaments, the feudal lord spent his time hunting. Guided by the huntsmen, the entire party charged into the thicket at a sign from King Meladius. Young Tristan galloped along by his side with the utmost assurance; next to him rode the faithful Curvenal, who lavished all manner of advice on his young protégé. Following the bloodthirsty hounds, the horsemen plunged into the mysterious forest in pursuit of a stag: all of a sudden, two armed men emerged from behind the pines. They had been lying in wait for the king. Without the slightest provocation, they thrust their spears into his body and left him dead on the ground. Curvenal barely had time to fling himself in front of Tristan to protect him, before the killers vanished into the dense foliage.

Coe le roy meliad° vn iour qil estoit ale chacier fu octis
p · iij · chlis de · coz · et eult octis son filz tristan siez
eussent congneu et coe gouuinal lemena dens le
roy de gaule pour doubte de sa marrastre qi le haoit. xxbiij

En telle maniere fu destournee la
marrastre tristan de mourir et
par tristan meismes la ou elle
lui pourchacoit se mort de tout
son pouoir Et sachies que ceste
chose que tristan fist par son con
seil et par son sens lui fu tournee
a grant valour et a trop grant bonte de tous les
sages hommes et de tous les preudommes de loenoz.
Et dirent les vns et les autres coument quil

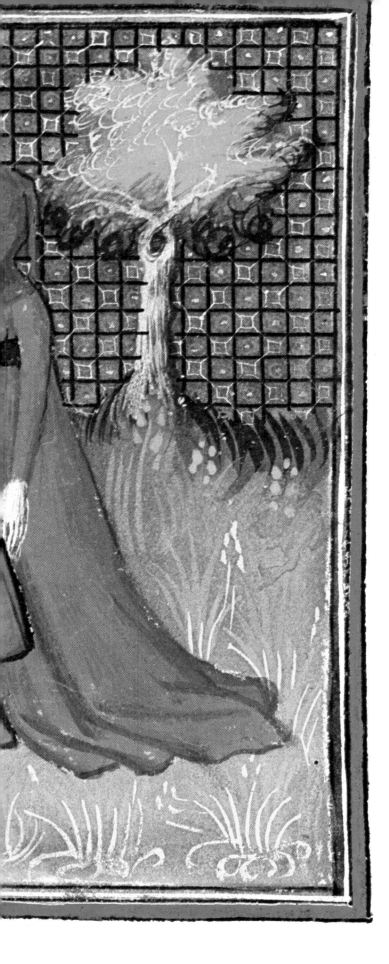

Tension was high at the court of Faramont, King of France: his daughter had fallen in love with the handsome Tristan, who had taken refuge there with Curvenal, whose sole pastimes were fencing, playing the harp and the intricacies of the chess-board. The damsels of the court cast longing glances towards the supremely eligible sixteen-year-old, while Princess Belide sought vainly to lure him into her bed. But Tristan ignored these intrigues, which, in any case, had not escaped the watchful eye of the sollicitous Curvenal. Alas, Belide's love soon changed to hatred. Our hero found himself hauled before the king, hands bound, to answer to charges of having raped the princess. In the presence of the king, holding the symbol of his royal power, the unsheathed sword, Curvenal and Belide simultaneously argued their cases in a exceedingly heated trial which came close to a form of judicial combat. Yet the arm of Belide, held out accusingly, must have trembled at the thought of the danger now threatening the one whom, despite everything, she still loved.

Together with Curvenal, who followed him like his shadow, Tristan had reached Cornwall, where, like the true knight that he was, his first act was to go and pay homage to the lord of the land, King Mark, a bearded old man surrounded by a swarm of courtiers who were looking forward anxiously to the moment of his death, so as to be able to bid for the royal crown. Tristan found him outside the walls of the castle of Tintagel, seated in the midst of a meadow bright with spring flowers; he promptly knelt before his majesty, his arms spread out as a sign of trusting submission. He swore allegiance to him, and, watched nervously by two courtiers, the king extended a paternal welcome to the newcomer, doubtless deeply touched by such spontaneous emotion. Imagine their astonishment when they eventually discovered that Tristan was really the nephew of King Mark, and a very tough competitor for the throne of Cornwall!

As the result of a wound which had become poisoned, Tristan was treated with these simple folk remedies. Alas! plasters and ointments alike were powerless to check the violent poison coursing through his veins. The sturdy young man felt his strength ebb; he grew paler from day to day, till his clumsy fingers could scarcely wrest from his harp a few chords which only expressed his grief.

A lady well versed in the art of healing advised him to go and seek a cure overseas. A boat was found, and some food, with his harp was loaded on board, under a canvas to protect him from rain, wind and sun. Before the king and Curvenal, both in tears, and the feigned distress of the jealous courtiers, the solitary moribund figure was placed aboard, and the craft was set loose, into the benevolent custody of the winds.

No sooner than he had been cured by the magic herbs of Isolde the Fair, daughter of the King of Ireland, Tristan set off once more on his wanderings, on horseback, through the misty forests of the country, ready to oppose whatever armed stranger might stand across his path. By the hearth of the castle, during the long evenings, he sang epic songs on his harp, and the attentive ears of the persons living at the court were touched by the tales of the exploits of a man who could never be defeated.

Behold him, all clad in white, his face hidden under his helmet, galloping on his caparisoned charger towards the tournament at which his bravery was to enable him to challenge and fell, before the admiring gaze of his beauty, the rival who had bid against him for the heart of Isolde the Fair...

Tristan, the white knight, the breaker of shields and lances, hammerer of armor, had just beaten his rival a second time in the lists, while Isolde watched from her window. For fear he might be recognised, he quickly dodged away, keeping the visor of his helmet lowered, and slipped into the forest, to await the coming of nightfall. Near a fountain where he had stopped to quench his thirst, he had laid down his coat of mail, his shield, his helmet and his gauntlets. He had tied his charger to a pine tree, keeping only his trusty sword ready at his waist—the forest could spring the most unpleasant surprises on the unwary knight! Counting his bruises with each step, Tristan then went back to the royal castle like a common marauder, with the complicity of the night which enabled him to return, unrecognised, to the room where Curvenal awaited him.

At the court of King Mark, life was one long succession of feasting, jousting and amorous intriguing. A lady from a nearby hamlet who was loved by the king suddenly fell in love with the brilliant Tristan. His confidant was a misshapen dwarf with a bushy beard, a creature from a fairy tale, whose wisdom was beyond question. It is he who could be seen leading Tristan in his broad-sleeved red cloak to the rose of Cornwall, his mistress, not without betraying her and confessing to King Mark the place where they were to meet. In this way the dwarf's spite caused members of one and the same family to clash in bloody combat; when it was over, both of them were much the worse for wear: Tristan dragging himself along with his last remaining strength to reach his lady's bed, and the king returning to Tintagel.

King Mark was getting old, his beard was now grey. It was time for him to marry, in the hope of leaving an heir, if only to silence the jealous barons and assure the succession to the throne of Cornwall. He shared his feelings with Tristan, who swore to find him the ideal woman. Had he not spoken most approvingly of the beauty of Isolde the Fair, whose hair was so diaphanous that, when caught in a sunbeam, it looked like a piece of gold? There could be no doubt that returning to Ireland meant enduring the storm-tossed sea and confronting a hostile feudal world. But it did not matter: Tristan could not depart from his oath. Together with Curvenal and an escort, he set sail on a richly adorned vessel, and the winds of Cornwall sweeping down from the cliffs soon swelled his white sail.

At the Irish court Tristan's prowess had silenced the age-old hatred, and King Hanguin could only be pleased with the services of a poet-knight whose sword defeated his enemies and whose harp charmed the ladies of the court, including the radiant Isolde the Fair. Moreover, the care which he needed in his declining years and his fear of ever drawing his sword again caused him to stay well away from the lists. Should a rival come to challenge the king to a judicial combat, Tristan was the one who, wearing the royal cloak with its three crowns, his face masked by a helmet, rode forward to do battle on his behalf. Under the watchful gaze of the two kings acting as judges, leaning on the balustrade, the fight began; Tristan, holding his long sword in both hands, had just struck his first blow which landed right on his opponent's skull.

Ireland had now been left far behind, as the young man joyfully returned with the beautiful promised bride to King Mark. His eyes dwelt longingly on the womanly shapes which could be discerned under her long robes; his heart was heavy with regret at the thought of abandoning the beautiful Isolde, whom he had conquered, to the bed of his uncle. But away with sly thoughts! The sea was beautiful and life on board ship reminded him of the splendid living at court. On the strings of his harp Tristan played a plaintive melody, or, leaning over the chess table, he followed Isolde's hands as they ran across the board. One day, as they were approaching Cornwall, the winds dropped, the sun beat down hotter and hotter, and the white-sailed vessel became becalmed near a row of cliffs. Everyone was thirsty and called for water to drink. Through a misunderstanding which Fate must surely have willed, Curvenal and Brangane, Isolde's lady companion, offered the two young people the golden goblets containing the magic potion which gave love to those who drank it. It had been jealously kept for King Mark and his young bride. At once, the loyalty of our chivalrous hero vanished. Tristan's eyes stared ever more insistently into those of Isolde the Fair, while his hands touched hers in an embrace which was to seal for ever the great passion which devoured the two lovers.

Tristan's valor and Isolde's beauty had enabled the love-struck mariners to triumph over all their enemies and to find the soil of Cornwall, where, in the midst of the glittering royal court, the wedding of Mark and Isolde was soon to be held.

The heroes of the day stood together under the porch of the royal chapel. Wearing golden crowns the royal couple stood side by side, Mark wearing a full red cloak lined with vair, Isolde in a pink robe embroidered in gold. Between them, the priest in his blue cape blessed their joined hands while reading from the ritual of the sacramental texts. Behind the king, in a green coat, Tristan shared with Curvenal the anguish which afflicted him, while Brangane, loyal to the point of sacrifice, leaned over the bride, apparently imagining the hours which awaited her in the royal bedchamber, with the complicity of the night.

Dramatic events at the court of Cornwall: Isolde the Fair had been abducted by a knight from King Arthur's court. Tristan, on his way back to the palace from a new series of adventures, found the atmosphere unbearably heavy: King Mark, shattered by this blow of Fate, was surrounded by hypocritical courtiers whose sidelong glances suggested the worst about the queen's fidelity. Without even descending from his charger, Tristan merely lifted the visor of his helmet to reply to King Mark. The king, in turn, his arms raised imploringly, then sent him forth to find the queen. Accompanied by Curvenal, and with his lance at the ready, our lover rode off without delay following the tracks of the man who had kidnapped his beauty.

Wearing a blue cloak, King Mark rested in his armchair, in the shade of a pine. He was tired of the poisonous life of the Cornish court, of its endless whispered innuendo about the virtue of the ladies and the fidelity of Isolde, whom Tristan had just brought back to Tintagel. He was deep in these morbid thoughts when, suddenly, a knight and his lady appeared before him and presented him with a magic horn: no unfaithful lady could ever drink from it without spilling its contents over her dress. It was decided that all the ladies of the court, including the noblest of them all, Isolde, would undergo this test. Alas! the wine spilled over her, but King Mark, anxious not to lose her, accepted her protestations of innocence, much to the discomfort of the jealous barons.

Having finally been convicted of adultery, to the immense grief of King Mark, the lovers were delivered to the royal tribunal: Tristan was to be burnt alive, and Isolde sent to live among the lepers. While he was being taken to the place of execution Tristan escaped from his warders and took Isolde with him. The two fugitives reached the depths of the forest of Morrois so as to be quite safe. After galloping for many hours through the brush they came to the towering gates of a castle. They parleyed for a while under the white walls, but soon the charms of Isolde, seated on her white horse, moved the lord of the castle to open up and offer the two young people and their friends hospitality. Far from the bustle of the court, the days and nights went by happily for the lovers, while Curvenal stood guard at their door to keep away the indiscreet gaze of strangers.

Tristan, a hunted man, and sick to boot, had found refuge in Little Britain with King Hoel and his daughter Isolde of the White Hands. She too was familiar with the virtues of magic herbs, and soon Tristan, having recovered his strength and looks, performed so many exploits in the service of his new master that he offered the young man the hand of his daughter. Faithful to the memory of Isolde the Fair, Tristan doubtless accepted this official union as a friend, without actually having to share the bed of the young bride. On a flowery lawn our heroes held hands, while, in the background, Curvenal and Kaedin, the princess's brother, promised to watch over the newlyweds and to do everything to make Tristan forget Isolde the Fair.

The adventurous life held many surprises for the young knight, who thought only of battle and the clash of swords. Tristan defeated all the enemies of King Hoel, while Isolde of the White Hands, in her bedchamber, vainly awaited her husband to whom she was to offer her flower. Then, one day, he met the giant Nabon, whose heavy club crushed the skulls of all those rash enough to confront him. Tristan armed himself with a club for the first time, studied his opponent's manner of fighting, and managed to fell Nabon with a mighty blow on the helmet. As Tristan's club rose

for another blow, the giant lay helplessly on the grass, unable to reach his huge sword.

With the visor of his helmet raised and his distinctive three-crown emblem easily recognisable, Tristan received a letter from Isolde the Fair. While Brangane, who had brought it to him, stood by, he nervously opened the seal and read the message within: "Dear Tristan, you have brought me pain and sadness." At his side stood his brother-in-law Kaedin, wearing a red doublet; he was doubtless worried lest the arrival of this letter, borne by the young lady in the white headdress, might revive the fatal passion of which he had penetrated the deadly secret. His friendship for Tristan was such that he knew full well that neither the exploits which lay ahead nor the love of his sister, the virgin-wife, would stop the bold young lover from replying to Isolde the Fair. With their gaze fixed on the castle of Tintagel, now visible on the horizon, the brothers-in-law quickly rode off towards Cornwall.

One day, King Arthur had ridden into a dense forest, the abode of a monster with the head of a snake and the body of a cat, and which made the most frightful barking noises. At court everyone began to worry about his prolonged absence. Several knights rode out to find him, among them Tristan, the hero with the three crowns. For weeks on end he carefully peered into the undergrowth looking for the lost king. Suddenly, he came across an incredible sight: in a clearing two strange knights were holding King Arthur down while a woman of terrifying aspect raised a large sword with which she was about to cut off his head. Before they could even think of running away, Tristan felled the two attackers, and the king, who had by now recovered from his fright, killed the sinister lady.

Having found Isolde the Fair at the castle of Tintagel, while travelling incognito, Tristan had to return to the forest. From one refuge to the next he sadly made his way. His complexion became so livid that a young woman took pity on him and accompanied him as far as a hospitable manor house. While the knight was resting in the room set aside for him, she came with her harp and sang sentimental plaintive ballads. He was so deeply moved by her song that the color came back into his cheeks and he was at last able to prop himself on one elbow, as he listened to a love song which he himself had composed while a fugitive, with Isolde the Fair, in that same forest where he was now wandering alone. His grief rose to such a pitch that he lost all control of himself and ran out of the house like a madman.

The vast forest, deep in the heart of Cornwall, still resounded to the plaintive tones of Tristan who was lamenting his unrequited love. Not wishing to meet him, King Mark took care to steer his hunting parties in some other direction, while the fugitive's brother-in-law, together with Palamede, was out looking for him. One evening they reached a fountain. Weary from their travels, they hung their swords and their shields from two broad leaved trees, and, leaning on the rim of the well, they soon confessed their love for Queen Isolde, without ever uttering her name. Like Tristan, both of them were ensnared by the same amorous passion.

At Tintagel Isolde the Fair was desperately unhappy ; Brangane spent most of her time consoling her. King Mark knew that she had seen Tristan clandestinely, yet his affection for the guilty young lovers was such that he could not bring himself to take his vengeance on his spouse. One day, on returning to the castle after a long day's hunt, he heard the sound of Isolde's harp coming from a corner of the garden, where she sat singing plaintively of the grief she was suffering on account of a jealous baron: Tristan had been found dead in the forest. Mark moved closer. Could Isolde have noticed him ? In her blue, open-necked robe she continued her lament, telling how she was going to join Tristan in the other world where lovers were reunited. Now thoroughly disconcerted, the king gave orders that she was to be watched closely every minute of the day.

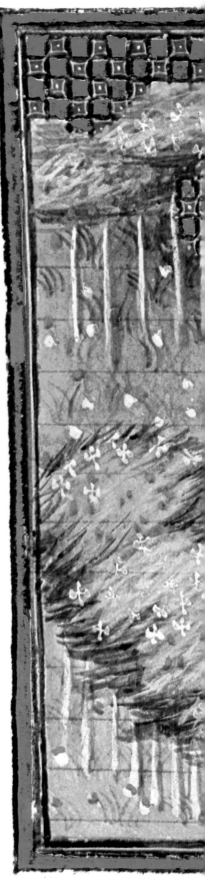

Throughout their adventurous lives, the knights had to face all sorts of trials and dangers, each more unexpected than the last. In order to force their way into a walled hamlet, one of them had to cross three bridges, the first of which was guarded by two brothers who promptly charged at the newcomer, lance in hand. One of the defenders was already prostrate on the ground, his bloodied face next to the hoofs of his warhorse; his companion, meanwhile, found himself unseated by a thrust of the lance deftly aimed at the visor of his helmet.

In the misty Breton forests, rarely did a day go by without some encounter in which one's knightly honor had to be defended by force of arms or one had to force one's way through against tremendous odds: failure on such occasions meant a badly mangled body enclosed in a dented coat of mail. Whenever two friends happened to meet, therefore, it was truly a joyous event: they would embrace warmly without even bothering to alight from their horses. The trees in bloom served as a fitting background to the happiness which could be seen in their faces.

Kaedin had received a message from Isolde the Fair. Far from returning his love, she proved to be cruel to the brother-in-law of Tristan. "Madness is not vassalage," were the words she wrote to him. Overwhelmed by this categorical verdict, the knight took refuge in solitude, without eating or drinking for three days and nights; he even forsook his harp, whose gentle tones could still have tempered his grief. He lay on the ground in his voluminous red cloak and handed the blue-coated messenger the scroll which would prove to Isolde the Fair that he had allowed himself to die out of love for her.

As he wandered through the Morrois forest in his deranged state, Tristan killed the giant Taulas who had been terrorising the country all around. The people, in an outpouring of joy, led the madman who had saved them to the royal court, where his dog alone recognised him, such were the marks left on his features by his sufferings. However, the care lavished on him by the compassionate Isolde caused his beauty to return and those around him began to recognise him once more. Tristan thus had to leave Cornwall; King Mark, on his white charger, together with the barons with the sly smile, escorted him until they were met by the knight with the golden crown, a friend who was to accompany Tristan into exile.

The two companions intended to ride as far as the land of King Arthur and to meet the knights of the Round Table. They spent their days galloping along on their chargers, each of which was clad in a long emblazoned shabrack, and their nights wrapped up in their cloaks under the broad forest canopy. Their journey had been uneventful until, one day, they came to a stone bridge and found their path blocked by two knights who had emerged from the forest

at the same time as them. The threatening manner of the two strangers made a clash inevitable. Tristan was the first to spur his mount forward: he lunged at his adversary's chest with his lance and knocked him to the ground with the first blow. Dinadan attacked the second knight and, after a struggle, left him dead on the ground.

But the trials of the two friends were not over. No sooner had they recovered from the excitement of the last encounter than they were confronted by thirty knights who had been sent out by Morgain, King Arthur's sister, to pursue Lancelot. They thought they had recognised their quarry and promptly went into action. Seeing that they were heavily outnumbered, Dinadan hesitated, but Tristan rebuked him so severely in the name of feudal honor that he agreed to draw his heavy sword and wield it in battle. A terrible struggle then took place, in which the two companions faced tremendous odds. Thanks to Tristan's new-found strength their adversaries bit the dust, one after the other, until the survivors took to their heels. Our heroes were then able at last to cross the bridge, on their way to new adventures.

cōmēt meſk triſtã trou
ua ḳeux le ſeneſchal ⁊ ſei
gremoꝛ ⁊ cōmēt il iou
ſta ꝯtre culꝛ ⁊ les abati. li
Eue triſtan ne reſpont
uiē apawle que oÿ naꝺa᷑
luẏ ꝺie ains met tout :
mamtenant leſai ꝺeuant

After Dinadan had left to go back to King Arthur's court, Tristan found himself once more alone. His visor poised to slam shut at a moment's notice, the young knight of the three crowns went on his way along the forest paths, eager for new encounters which could enhance his renown. One evening he came to a fountain where two knights were resting, their weapons hung on stakes and their horses tied to a post. A clash was inevitable. In keeping with feudal custom Tristan waited until his two adversaries had mounted their chargers before challenging them. After breaking the first knight's lance, he unhorsed the second, and then rode on his way.

Tristan had just spent the night as the guest of Persides, in his father's fortress. Next morning, he was relaxing with his hosts when, all of a sudden, a large troop of armed men appeared before the castle walls. Despite his aged host's entreaties, Tristan promptly reached for his weapons and armor and, followed by his companion, went to the stables. Having ordered the raising of the portcullis, the two young men charged out, with lowered visors, to confront the newcomers. Their leader, his face exposed and his hand raised as a sign of peace, did his best to restrain the hot-headed knight of the golden crowns, suspecting that he might be King Mark's nephew. But his efforts were to no avail: a fight broke out, and the two knights, notwithstanding their courage, were soon overpowered.

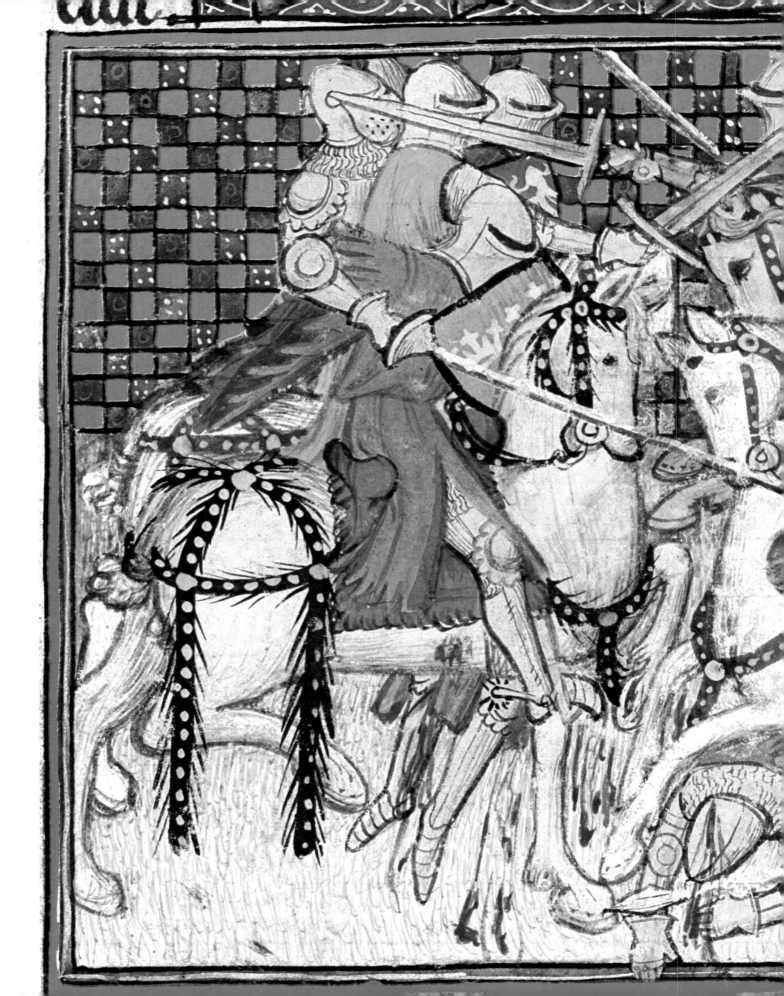

The kind of fighting that went on at the tournaments was a deadly serious affair, in which a knight could be seriously injured in a variety of ways, or could even lose his life. Adversaries sometimes challenged each other angrily, denouncing a knight's cowardice, weakness or honor as the case may be, and then proceeding to resolve the issue in fierce hand-to-hand combat. Tristan certainly did not regard such clashes as sporting events; in the heat of the action, the green knight regularly unhorsed his opponents, ran them through with his lance or smashed their skulls with his heavy sword.

During the free-for-all which took place below the castle walls, Tristan was knocked over by an adversary who had taken him by surprise. Enraged by this mishap and mortified at the thought that his renown might thus be tarnished in the world of chivalry, perhaps as far away as Cornwall, he swiftly leapt back into the saddle and fled from the scene of the fighting. Spurred on by this display of cowardice, a whole host of enemies now began to chase him, eager, now that he was evidently tired, to avenge past humiliations. Their hopes were dashed, however, as the green knight, his pride stung to the quick, soon forgot his fatigue and dispatched his pursuers one by one.

The vast gloomy forests often attracted knights and sovereigns who were eager to enhance their warlike reputations and who wandered about in the quest for worthy adversaries. One of them, with a crowned helmet, attacked a knight with a richly feathered helmet, whose three-pronged lance was thrust across his path.

In her castle at Tintagel, Isolde the Fair was worried about Tristan's prolonged absence and his silence. She sent Brangane's niece, with a squire, out to seek news of her loved one; the young girl's candor was to serve her well in her quest for information and would disarm many a knight whom she encountered along the way. One day, however, she was taken hostage by the giant known as "Merciless", who was not at all impressed by her innocence. Having first killed her squire, he then dragged her off into the undergrowth, when, all of a sudden, a young knight appeared, followed by his two squires. At the first sound of clashing swords the giant fled.

Care-worn and haggard, Tristan had found refuge in a small castle whose chamberlain, a former knight, took pity on the evident distress of this brother-in-arms; he took care of his horse and weapons before leading him to his room for the night. Some armed men who had been sent out to hunt down the knight with the three crowns also found their way to the castle gates; one of them, taller than the rest, with a bushy beard, sent his squire to ask the lord of the house if he had seen anything unusual. A valet, with raised hand, persuaded him that his master lived in the modest dwelling alone.

One day, when King Mark was out hunting a big stag, Isolde found herself alone in her country residence of Tolan. Brangane's niece still had not come back with news of Tristan, whom she awaited impatiently all day and all night. Then, as if in response to her most fervent desire, a servant announced the arrival of the knight with the three bird emblem, who was anxious to see for himself the beauty of Isolde of whom he had heard Tristan speak so often, and to bring her news of her banished lover. No sooner had he entered the room than he weakened at the knees with emotion at the sight of the princess in her long orange robe. Restraining her own emotion, she asked him to rise and tell her his message.

King Mark had heard a rumor which suggested that Tristan was hiding somewhere in Cornwall waiting for an opportunity to overthrow his uncle. The knights-errant who stopped at the royal castle were questioned and watched during their stay, unknown to the queen. One of them had just left the residence of Tolan, and it suddenly occurred to King Mark that he might be spying for Tristan. He promptly sent his men out after him, with orders to hunt him down mercilessly. The king himself sent for his charger with the blue lion emblem and mounted it, while two squires carrying his crowned helmet and his scepter waited at his side before leaving with him.

Comment le roy mair qui moult estoit dou
lant de mort yuain aur blanches mains qui a
uoit abatu deux de ses cheualiers sarma, et espia
le dit yuain au partir de tintaiol. lxiij.

N ceste partie dit le conte :
que trois iours entiers demo
ura messire yuain aur blan
ches mains en la maison du
roy mairch, et lors se partirent
la qui yroit cheuauchant
par le royaume de cornuail
le pour sauoir seul pourroit
en aucune maniere apprendre nouuel

Having searched in Cornwall for Tristan, who was thought to be carrying a black shield, but failing to find him, the two knights crossed the sea once more and reached the land of Logres, the kingdom of King Arthur. One evening they came across a building with pink walls, which they took to be a friendly hospitable place. In fact it was here that Tristan and two other knights were being held prisoner. Daras, the lord of the house, came out to meet them and let them stay in his house for two days, with their squires, without ever allowing them to suspect the presence of the prisoners.

In their prison with its four towers the three knights lamented over their sorry plight, and expected at any minute to be beheaded. Tristan, with the three-crown emblem on his shield, did his best to revive the spirits of his companions by his witty reflections on the effect of prison life, which "tames the criminal and makes the proud man humble". Daras, their captor, was far from being as cruel as they imagined him to be; shortly they were to be set free, for the greater honor of chivalry and not out of pity for these three wanderers.

Wearing a blue tunic and a green cap, Tristan rode unarmed to the land of Logres, in the company of two squires. Few people would have recognised the hot-headed Tristan, hero of endless battles, under this bland and peaceful exterior. The lookout posted on the tower of the castle of Morgain, sister of King Arthur, had spotted the three travellers and noticed their disarming manner. He sent word to the princess, who ordered one of her courtiers to meet them at the gate.

On the orders of King Arthur a tournament was to be held, with many knights from Scotland and Ireland, outside the walls of the castle of the Hard Rock. Morgain made this announcement to her guests in the hope of discovering the champion who could avenge the persecution of her royal brother—and who had always eluded her as a result of the spells cast by the magician Merlin, who was now dead. The newcomers spent the night coming to an agreement on how to act, and, in the morning, Tristan revealed his name to her, and declared himself ready to uphold her honor. Morgain then handed to her herald the large green shield which was symbolically adorned with an effigy of a knight standing proudly with each of his feet on a royal head.

Unrecognisable under his helmet, the knight with the strange green shield felled his adversaries one after the other. In the royal box, Queen Guinevere and the ladies marveled at such brilliance. King Arthur, for his part, was particularly intrigued by the figure on the shield; he felt in no mood to tangle with the stranger in the lists. Therefore, once the jousting was over, he went with his men to lie in wait at the edge of the forest which Tristan had to cross on his way home. The young man suddenly appeared, in the company of his faithful Curvenal, whom he had found miraculously, proudly carrying the shield of one of his victims at the end of his lance. He assured the king that he knew nothing of courtly intrigues and refused to reveal his identity. As the royal escort seemed reluctant to let them through, Tristan and Curneval had to act forcibly in order to proceed on their way, unhorsing the king and his retinue in the process.

Fate had ordained that the protagonists of the legend, Tristan, the lover of Isolde the Fair, and Lancelot, lover of Guinevere, should meet, without recognising each other, in the presence of Curvenal. From the very first blow they sensed that they were equally matched; thereafter they broke each other's lances to no avail. Both of them, once they had been thrown from the saddle, fought on using the stump of their weapons, but neither of them fell. Eventually the knight who was once more carrying his shield with the three-crown emblem, and his adversary in the red cloak, found themselves face to face, unarmed, and also unbeaten. They removed helmets as a sign of a truce, and identified themselves. Overcome with joy, they embraced warmly, exchanging swords as a gesture of courtesy; Lancelot, who was delighted to have found Tristan at long last, took him to King Arthur's court.

After his victories at the tournament of the Hard Rock, the fame of Tristan at the royal court was such that he was promptly given a seat at the Round Table, with the inscription "The Seat of Tristan". Regardless of the concern he felt at the presence of Lancelot, the sovereign was proud to be host to the two most famous knights in the world. Tristan took the customary oath, undertaking to do his utmost to enhance the honor of the Round Table, and to refrain from fighting against it except in formal competition. Within a few days the entire court was aware of the countless exploits of its new guest.

Meanwhile, at Tintagel, King Mark, constantly goaded by the jealous barons, sought the death of Tristan, and pondered over ways of seizing the young man who was being granted such honors at the court of King Arthur. Being anxious to avoid an armed clash with him, however, he entrusted the government of the kingdom to one of his favorites; then, disguised as a pilgrim, he went with his retinue to the land of Logres. Wearing his gold-crowned helmet he easily disposed of those knights who happened to obstruct his path; indeed, his squires scarcely managed to keep his weapons and armor in proper condition to cope with any surprise encounter. One day, however, a particularly tough opponent came along: having begun on horseback, the duel continued on foot, with swords, until King Mark finally succumbed.

King Mark and his retinue, still hunting for Tristan, were moving along a valley when they were suddenly attacked by three knights seeking vengeance for the murder of the father of one of them, which they supposed was the work of the sovereign. The engagement started badly: the king was knocked to the ground, and only the intervention of his escort saved him and unhorsed the three aggressors. The defeated knights, prostrate on the ground, begged for mercy. Mark, in

his rage, ripped off their leader's helmet, beat his head with the pommel of his sword, and was on the point of chopping it off altogether when a member of his escort, seizing the blade of the royal sword, reminded him that it was wrong, under the code of chivalry, to strike an unarmed man.

Six knights of the Round Table were on their way back to the court of King Arthur. Tired and thirsty after their adventures, they halted at a fountain, hung their weapons and shields on the trees, took off their armor and were just about to quench their thirst when King Mark and his retinue appeared on the scene. Finding them thus unprepared he could scarcely challenge them to battle. The monarch, who, only moments before, had been boasting to his companions of a multitude of exploits, thus took the precaution of avoiding a confrontation. In any case, he was reluctant to wait and possibly make new enemies while he was still digesting the splendid meal he had had at a castle along the way.

The knights of the Round Table, once they had quenched their thirst and rested, set out on their way and, as could be expected, ran into the retinue of King Mark after riding at full speed. In the meantime they had been joined by King Arthur's clown; they dressed him in a suit of armor and armed him with a stake so that he could join in the fighting. The ensuing engagement was a fierce one. When it was all over, they found themselves herded like captives before the clown, who lay on the ground moaning with pain from his injuries, and asking themselves a great number of questions about the identity of this madman from the forests who had just beaten all seven of them.

A medieval hamlet, its pink surrounding walls crowned by battlements and machicolated towers. The castle in the middle belonged to Morgain, King Arthur's sister; despite all the monarch's efforts to crush his rebellious younger sister, the castle still had not been vanquished. On the flower-strewn meadow which stretched along the foot of the wall an armed knight stood, his lance at the ready, watching over the two adversaries whom he had just overpowered, while ready at the same time to repel some other intruders who had appeared on the left. Who were they? No one knew. The ladies were soon to watch from the battlements, oblivious to all but the prowess of their champion.

After spending a pleasant month at the court of King Arthur, where gallantry was combined with honors, King Mark expressed a desire to return to Cornwall. He took his leave of Queen Guinevere, after swearing to the king, his host, on the Holy Writ, that Tristan would be granted the fullest pardon and that he would be readmitted to the court. Some of those present were happy to see unity thus restored to a family which had long been divided by Fate, while others were disturbed by this oath, which they felt was insincere. Indeed, Lancelot, when taking his leave, warned Tristan against his uncle's falseness.

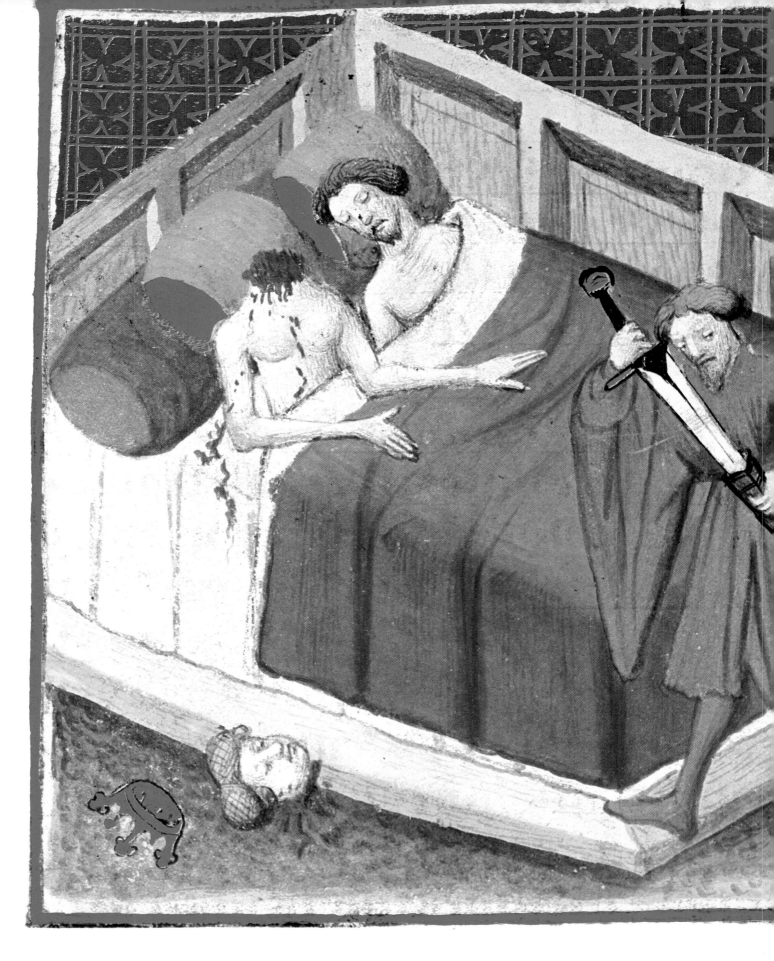

In her castle of the Black Rock the Queen of Orcania had agreed to reward the knight who won a tournament by offering to share with him the warmth of her royal bed. Tired after a long night of love, the two casual lovers were still sleeping peacefully at daybreak. At that moment, the Queen's son happened to come across this intimate scene. Clearly he could not dispatch an unarmed knight, as that was forbidden by the code of chivalry; but his act of matricide seemed fully justified by the disgrace which his mother had heaped upon her children by her foul deed. He drew his long sword and, just as his mother was awakening, he sliced off her head, which rolled on to the floor, next to the royal crown. Then, returning his sword to its scabbard, he left the bedroom without so much as waking the sleeping knight.

85

King Arthur was holding a council meeting on the grounds of the castle, in the company of three favorites, when the arrival of a messenger was announced: it was the same woman that had been sent by Queen Isolde to find her lover. She handed Lancelot two letters from Tristan, one for the king and the other for himself. Both were written in the form of a ballad, as an expression of friendship and gratitude. Lancelot promptly went to join the king and his councillors in the castle grounds and, on bended knee, he handed him Tristan's letter, while the lady who had brought the message looked on approvingly.

King Mark and Queen Isolde the Fair were holding their court at Tintagel, surrounded by their kinfolk, who were ever watchful in case some evidence of infidelity on the part of their queen should come to light. Tristan, who had been wounded in action, was recovering from his injuries in a nearby castle.

A manservant suddenly announced that the Saxons had landed during the night, and, after burning their boats, were invading Cornwall. Well aware of their warlike character, and alarmed at the thought that Tristan was not present, King Mark summoned his councillors, and, under heavy escort, he sent the queen away from Tintagel to the safety of a fortress. The barons immediately sent a messenger to Tristan, who being a faithful vassal, could not ignore his suzerain's appeal, despite his injuries. He therefore came and knelt before him, to the evident relief of the king's councillors.

The fighting with the Saxons was merciless, with terrible losses on both sides. As was his wont, Tristan performed prodigious feats of arms; and, although in the heat of battle he had already forgotten his wounds, he never lost sight of his duty to protect his uncle, who was hard pressed, deep in the fray. He suddenly noticed a Saxon striking a huge blow at the monarch's left shoulder, knocking him to the ground, where he lay helpless and surrounded by enemies. Followed by a knight, Tristan rushed to the spot and hacked out a clearing in the midst of the enemy force, cracking many a lance and helmet in the process.

tant laisse ore le compte a parler deule tretô
ne au roy march ↑ et mout tristan pour de
uiser cômment il esplorterent contre les saisnes

Coment mess tristan que il oc trette la bataille
aux saines de ple roy marc fuz le soir ardoir leur
mainere et côe il le porta bn ala bataille et relcom
le roy marc ôles saines auoient abatu .iiij. U.

E compte dit que quant le messa
ge de lolt de saulloigne se fu party
de tintagel Apres ce quil fut acer
tene de par mout tristan que les
saisnes auoient la bataille ain
sy comme vous auez oy ca arrie
res et mous tristan parole au roy march ↑ luy
dist · Sire il me semble que bon seroit afaire pô

On the evening of the battle the men of Cornwall, realising that their king was injured, sought to come to terms with the Saxons and agreed to pay them tribute. However, Tristan came along at that precise moment, and proposed to fight the Saxon chief Helyas single-handed, in order to spare the country the shame of defeat. The challenge was accepted. The next day an enclosure was built and the two duellists found themselves face to face. With King Mark looking on anxiously, the fight began. As feint, thrust and parry followed each other in swift succession, Helyas realised that he would never get the better of his opponent. He eventually collapsed, and Tristan, seeing that he was unarmed, pardoned him, on condition that the Saxons should declare themselves vanquished.

Isolde the Fair, in a blue robe, and Tristan, who was wearing a green coat with the three-crown emblem, arrived at the gates of the castle of the Happy Guard, in Logres, at the head of a mounted party. What had happened?

The gossipmongers and the jealous barons vied with each other in devious attempts to surprise the two lovers in some compromising position, until, one day, Tristan, who had been made sleepy by a strong potion, was caught in the queen's bed and promptly imprisoned by order of the king. News of his arrest reached his friend Lancelot, who, in a series of adventures, managed to free him, abducting Isolde and taking both of them, with their retinue, to his castle, Happy Guard.

For several months the lovers met every night at their quarters at Happy Guard. Tristan spent the daylight hours hunting game in the surrounding forests, with Curvenal. He had just paused at a fountain to quench his thirst, when he noticed a monster with which he had already done battle, called the Barking Beast. He immediately sounded his horn to assemble his hounds; a knight who had been sent to Logres to find him came

running on hearing all the noise. It was Dinadan, who, not recognising King Mark's nephew, left the group of huntsmen, and, keenly disappointed, continued his quest.

One day, a knight who was looking for Tristan in the forest knocked on the door of Happy Guard Castle. In keeping with the law of hospitality to travelers, his horse was taken to a stable as soon as he dismounted, while the knight himself was given dinner and then ushered into the presence of the lady of the house, who was chatting to two of her ladies-in-waiting. Tristan, on learning of this untimely arrival, became suspicious and withdrew to the next room, pretending to need a rest. The stranger gave his name as Dinadan, and Isolde invited him to take his place by her side. As their conversation proceeded, the knight was deceived by the tone of familiarity which Isolde instantly showed towards him; actually she knew exactly why he had come and now did her best, without revealing her true identity, to make him forget his mission; she even persuaded him to take part, in her name, in a forthcoming tournament, wearing a helmet chosen by her.

Several hours away from the preceding scene, two knights, one of whom was Dinadan, rode towards that same tournament. They were discussing a rumor current in the land of Logres, about a unique treasure of chivalry and beauty which was said to exist at the castle of the Happy Guard. Dinadan, who had just come from there, promptly thought of Tristan and Isolde, whom he had not recognised. He was immersed in these thoughts when along came a knight who challenged him and his companions to combat, and unhorsed one of them, only to be himself thrown to the ground by a new arrival, Tristan, wearing a cloak adorned with gold crowns. The encounter concluded with mutual apologies and all four knights decided to go on to the tournament.

All around the lists where the jousting was to take place, tents had been put up for the knights and their companions. Isolde shared one of these with Tristan. They were watching a fight between a crowned head, King Herald of the Hundred Knights, and Dinadan, who was dressed in white and wearing the helmet given him by the queen. However, having been unhorsed, he was about to surrender the precious object to his conqueror, when Tristan, who had recognised Isolde's gift, stepped into the lists and forbade the king's squire to touch it. He ordered one of his men to pick it up before returning it to Dinadan.

In order to rest their weary and bruised limbs, the jousters sometimes went riding in the nearby forest, having first left their harnesses and weapons in the custody of their squires. Relaxing in their full courtly garments, they were trotting along calmly when they were suddenly confronted by the giant Brehus, who was known to be merciless towards any knight he met. At full gallop he lunged at the group of knights and treacherously struck Tristan in the back. Thanks to the swift reaction of a companion, who rode out in front of the giant's horse, thus throwing him to the ground, the four friends managed to escape from certain death.

Visitors to the castle of the Happy Guard were more and more numerous, especially after the announcement of a grand tournament which was to last several days. Palamede, who was still in love with Isolde the Fair, joined the throng in the secret hope of vanquishing Tristan and capturing from him the love of the queen. Just as the assembled knights were setting out for the tournament, along came King Galehodin, accompanied by four knights. Palamede, being anxious to impress those present, challenged him to a duel because he had found out that the monarch intended to abduct Isolde. He was determined to do his utmost, in the presence of the highly critical lovers, seated in their box with the ladies, to defeat his adversary.

The fighting on the first day lasted until nightfall. The ground on which the jousting had taken place had been literally plowed up by the hoofs of the chargers, and was now strewn with bits of lances, blades and shields—evidence of the violence of the action. Many of the knights who had been unhorsed had to surrender, and then withdraw to the tents to nurse their wounds. Even Tristan had to change weapons several times before he and his horse, clad entirely in red, returned to the fray.

Next day, no sooner had the royal trumpets sounded than the jousting started anew, and the fighting rapidly turned into a free-for-all. King Arthur leapt into the fray himself, together with Lancelot, in the hope that, unrecognised on account of his visor and his unmarked helmet, he could get close to the fascinating Isolde the Fair. His plan came unstuck, however, as Pala-

mede, guessing what he was about to attempt, unhorsed him directly in front of the queen, who was talking with her ladies-in-waiting. Two knights with lowered visors—one of them was Tristan—stood behind the royal party.

On the evening of the second day of the grand competition, Isolde, by now tired of the endless jousting, in which her lover was not always unscathed, withdrew to her pavilion with the red tiles. She was sitting down to table with her two ladies-in-waiting when King Arthur and Lancelot of the Lake, both of whom were eager to present their compliments to the lady of the house, appeared at the door. Tristan, forgetting the jealous impulses which at first surged in his breast, gave a joyous welcome to two men who had been his benefactors, and Isolde invited them to sit at table with the rest of the company.

fait a terre tout er. Et tant dônne le tant tel de
ce monseigneur tristan et tant a fait dycelui
glaiue que nul autre cheualier qui a doue fust
en la place nen peust plus faire.

ont tristan se porta bn le .iij. io^3 du tournoy et souuent
ceulx de la ptie du roy art^9 de cho bxz le ne seust tristan
ga h crier et dmad^{9}le toueret deus eulx et côe palamed
vint de hér tristan a la tente .lxix. v bj

E roy artus qui celui fait
uoit et quibien recoguoist
messire tristan le monstre
a lancelot et lui dit celui
est messire tristan qui la
besoigne a commancee par
deuers soy or regardôns
quil fera Car ie sçe tout
certamement qui vouldza luy faire meruel
les entrelui et palamedes feront proesces a el

The third day of the royal jousting saw Tristan and his men perform an impressive series of exploits, which were inspired doubtless as much by the thought of Isolde as by that of knightly honor. After he had felled two opponents, he then turned on King Arthur, who was riding a charger bedecked with golden crowns and distinguished by his royal helmet.

King Arthur had issued a proclamation throughout the kingdom saying that he was going to assemble all his vassals at a session of the court. As a knight of the Round Table, Tristan was on his way there, at Isolde's request, when Palamede, armed with a three-pronged lance, suddenly rode across his path. The image of the features of Isolde the Fair was uppermost in the minds of each of the knights, and a savage confrontation seemed inevitable. However, Palamede noticed that his adversary, his hair disheveled by the wind, was incompletely armed, and although challenged he decided to refrain from attacking him, in keeping with the laws of chivalry.

During the Whitsun festivities at Camelot, his royal city, King Arthur had made all the knights of the Round Table swear that they would set out on a quest for the Holy Grail for a year and a day— much to the discomfort of the ladies, who, for the duration, were forsaken by their husbands and lovers.

To avoid recognition, Tristan had his shield painted a single shade of green, and obeyed the old king, choosing not to return to the Happy Guard, in case he might be recognised there. One day, when he was at a fountain, just about to give his horse water, he met a stranger who

104

happened to be the son of Helyas, the Saxon whom he had beaten in a duel. A sword fight began, and the young man, abandoning all hope of defeating Tristan, allowed himself to be taken away into captivity.

Far, far away from Isolde, Tristan was out walking one day with Palamede in the midst of the flowers in bloom, wearing courtly dress. He now had his green shield with the distinctive three crowns. The two knights were chatting away, when a stranger wearing a white helmet and carrying a white shield suddenly appeared. Intending to put him at this ease, they invited him to undo and remove his helmet, whereupon Tristan recognised his friend Dinadan, who told him, amongst other things, of the exploits of a young knight named Galahad, son of Lancelot of the Lake, who had also been sent out to look for the Holy Grail.

Fully dedicated to the mission imposed on him by King Arthur, Tristan had not been back to the Happy Guard for several months. Now that Curneval had left him to take possession of the Kingdom of Lyoness, he was wandering alone. He therefore asked his friend Dinadan, whom he had just met, to go to Isolde, to take her news of his whereabouts in order to reassure her, and also to tell her to expect a visit from him soon.

Accompanied by two ladies-in-waiting, and suffering from the same anxiety that afflicts all women in love, the queen welcomed Dinadan who, on bended knee, con-

veyed to her the message sent by Tristan. She also knew that, despite all his promises, another year would certainly go by before she saw him again. So she prepared a reply for him in the form of a poem, "To you, my true, true friend", in which she expressed the full bitterness of separation.

Now involved in a new series of adventures, Tristan went on alone with his quest for the Holy Grail, though he felt that, on account of his guilty relationship with Isolde the Fair, it was unlikely he would ever be the one to discover it. After all, wasn't the successful knight supposed to be a man of pure heart, who had never told a lie? One day, at a crossroads, he met Palamede, the knight of the silver weapons, who com-

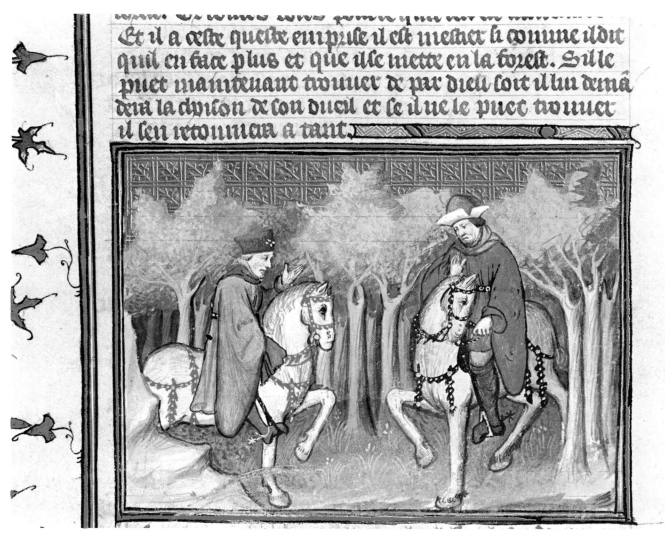

plained bitterly about the coldness shown to him by Isolde the Fair. Tristan listened to his complaints indulgently, warned him against the pitfalls of love, and, finally, the two rivals took their leave of each other.

In order to be left utterly alone, Isolde had a pavilion built near a fountain. Together with her ladies-in-waiting, she spent her days lamenting over Tristan's absence. A number of knights, attracted by her great beauty, came to visit her court. Two of them, Eric the Younger and Gawain, fought one day over her natural charms and, more particularly, over the slurs uttered by one of them against her good name. Their quarrel soon became exceedingly violent. Eric flung his adversary to the ground at the first blow, wounding him, so that Isolde's servants had to nurse him back to health before he could go on his way.

The search for the Holy Grail was a most demanding task; but Tristan was not to be deterred by anything, even the most unpleasant encounters. Once more reunited with his green shield bearing the distinctive three-crown emblem, he found himself doing battle, side by side with Palamede and another companion, against Harpin the Red, a chamberlain whose fortress could be seen in the background. Though two of his men were already on the ground, Harpin was determined to fight on. He charged at Palamede without noticing that Tristan's sword was fast approaching his helmet, which it then split down the middle.

While out walking in the forest, Palamede and Tristan discovered a superb stallion wandering about loose, without a master. They promptly began to look for him, and eventually found him asleep by a fountain, wrapped up in a large blue cloak. What a joy was theirs when they noticed that the knight was wearing Lancelot's sword! The three old friends began to talk; they joked about Tristan, rebuking him for seeking all the glory of battle for himself, whereas it should really go to the modest Palamede. Lancelot and his two friends then rose and went off on their quest.

Yet another lethal encounter had taken place: one of the few to escape unscathed was Tristan, who, holding on his left arm the shield of Palamede, supported with his arms the head of his injured friend and rival. On the ground lay their two adversaries, one of whom had been killed outright, still in the saddle, at the first blow. Tristan then took Palamede to the castle of the Tower of Pine, the home of the wife of the dead knight. Without telling her of her husband's death, he urged her to attend to the wounds of the dying Palamede.

A judicial duel was being fought in the presence of the Duke of Haudebort. who was sitting with his councillors. In the lists were Lancelot, carrying a white shield with red stripes, and Brunor, with a red shield. Lancelot sought vengeance for the death of a knight killed in combat, while Brunor was defending the honor of his brother, who had been unjustly charged with murder and imprisoned. But Lancelot, having noticed that his opponent was wielding Tristan's sword, decided to stop the fight, just when a knight intervened to announce that the knights should lay down their arms immediately, as there had been a misunderstanding.

In breach of the instructions received by all the knights of the Round Table, Tristan returned to the castle of the Happy Guard together with Brunor—another admirer of the queen—who was unaware of his companion's true identity. Without bothering to remove his armor the knight with the green shield clasped Isolde in his arms before the thoroughly startled ladies-in-waiting and the equally disconcerted Brunor, who now belatedly realised that he had unwittingly played into Tristan's hands. Even so, hospitality was not denied him at the Happy Guard, where the reunited lovers could not find it within them to resent unrequited affection.

The quest for the Holy Grail—a lofty ideal for men of warlike spirit—sometimes gave the knights involved certain experiences of an almost mystical nature. While he was resting on his shield in the Spoilt Forest, Lancelot felt a strange dizziness come over him; through a haze, he had glimpses of a pink chapel with blue tiles. Behind the iron grillwork of the gate he saw a large chandelier with six candles steadily burning before the goblet in the shape of a ciborium which was thought to contain the blood of Christ.

At the same time he discovered, near the chapel, a sick man lying on a tattered bed, his hands joined in prayer, begging for a cure through the divine mercy. As soon as Lancelot awoke the vision was gone—and he found himself once more alone in the forest.

During his solitary dreams Tristan imagined that he could see the castle of the Happy Guard in flames, and that Isolde was missing in the blaze, which had been set by a felon from Cornwall. In fact the premonition came true shortly afterwards. Having at last discovered the retreat of the lovers, King Mark landed with the Saxons in the land of Logres, laid waste the entire countryside and, in the absence of Tristan, entered the Happy Guard by surprise. Feeling pleased with himself, he left the castle with the woman who, for so long, had been absent from his palace and bed, while his knights subjected the entire place to fire and the sword. Before returning to Cornwall, the army laid siege to the royal city of Camelot, and King Mark himself mortally wounded King Arthur, whom he accused of having protected the two lovers.

The quest for the Holy Grail was a deadly perilous affair: indeed many a knight of the Round Table had already vanished into the depths of the enchanted forest, never to be seen again. Tristan himself one day encountered one hundred and fifty knights of unfriendly disposition and was left on the ground after the skirmish was over, presumed to be dead. He waited for night to fall, summoned up his remaining strength and dragged himself as far as an abbey, where an old monk took care of him for several months. His shield with the three crowns hung over his bed, he received a visit one day from three knights of the Round Table who were worried by his disappearance. The youngest of these, Galahad, the knight with the white shield, told him of the abduction of Isolde, the devastation which had been visited upon the city and the withdrawal of King Mark to Cornwall. Tristan was so distressed that he took more than a year to recover his health.

Having at last recovered his strength, Tristan left the abbey and went off to resume his adventures. He was furious at the thought that he had wasted so many years on the hopeless quest for the Holy Grail, and bitterly lamented having taken the oath prescribed by King Arthur, who had, for so many years, kept him from his loved one. He was determined to leave the land of Logres; yet, before leaving a country in which his courage had been tested so severely, he wanted to take one last look at the castle of the Happy Guard. While on his way there he found his path obstructed by a group of knights. Within moments, several of them were already scrambling desperately to escape from sudden death. With outstretched lance, Tristan charged at the last of them, lunging at his right shoulder in an attempt to unhorse him.

Tristan had returned to Cornwall, where he spent his days wandering through the forest that surrounded the castle of Tintagel. Life without Isolde was becoming unbearable: by devious means he managed to slip past the close surveillance of the jealous barons, even succeeding in spending some minutes with her. King Mark was still exceedingly worried; but, touched by the sufferings which his nephew had endured, he took him back, thus hoping to restore peace to a family which had for so many years been divided. Recovering his poetic talents, Tristan spent his days composing ballads and then singing them to the accompaniment of his harp. The barons, for their part, were busy amassing proof of persistent infidelity on the part of Isolde. The old king was beside himself with rage, and, one day while Tristan was singing a ballad to Isolde, who sat attentively on a cushion, he furtively entered the room and treacherously stuck a poisoned spear into the poet's side.

His crime committed, under the overwhelming impulse of jealousy, King Mark left the residence where the queen was living and returned to Tintagel followed by Andret, the evil nephew who had suggested the crime to him in the first place. Still carrying on his shoulder the poison-tipped lance, the king glanced knowingly at his accomplice, evidently quite satisfied with what he had done. As for the nephew, who was proud of his success, he reassured him with a gesture which could well have been that of the successor to the throne, because Isolde had borne him no heir, and the rival was now eliminated once and for all.

Tristan, now breathing his last, was taken to a closely guarded room in the palace. Every attention was shown to him, the very best of ointments were applied to his wound, a bandage was placed around his head in order to reduce his fever. During his more lucid moments Tristan called for Isolde, the only person capable of curing him, to come and touch his wound with the magic herbs from Ireland: but to no avail. Before expiring he said farewell to his faithful sword which had brought him such glory; he even managed to raise it slightly in a gesture of defiance as King Mark and his wife came into the room. With false compassion the monarch seemed to implore the dying knight's forgiveness, while, behind him, Isolde, seized by the most total feeling of desolation, showed that she was ready to join, in death, the loved one to whom Fate had inexorably tied her life.

Designed and produced by
Productions Liber SA
© Productions Liber SA,
and Editions Minerva SA
Fribourg - Genève, 1978/1986

Printed by
Printer Industria Gráfica
Barcelone, Espagne
Depósito legal : B. 9992-1986
Printed in Spain